PICTURES IN GLASS

William Fraser

Kangaroo Press

Front cover
Photographer: John Endacott

Reprinted 1992
First published in 1991 by Kangaroo Press Pty Ltd
3 Whitehall Road (P.O. Box 75) Kenthurst 2156
Typeset by G.T. Setters Pty Limited
Printed in Hong Kong by Colorcraft Ltd

ISBN 0 86417 392 X

Contents

Foreword

Its resurgence from the obscurity of a forgotten craft earlier this century has seen leadlighting become one of today's truly international crafts. Its popularity seems unbounded as more and more devotees learn the technique each year, with craftspersons all round the world setting up their own shops and studios.

The medium lends itself to the bold and imaginative use of original design graphics, endless combinations of form limited only by the artist's own vision.

Leadlighting is a visual craft and as such is able to transcend reality by the sensitive choice of subject matter and design, and the considered use of colour.

There is, and always will be, a strong demand in the market place for 'traditional' leadlights, works either copied from or based upon the recognised leadlight styles—including Victorian, Art Nouveau, Edwardian and Art Deco. Increasingly, however, there is also a demand for 'modern' leadlights, panels made with style and dramatic visual impact which will indelibly stamp themselves on the minds of future viewers as having been made in the latter part of the twentieth century.

Whereas previously churches and holy places used leadlights to depict aspects of humanity's spiritual life, today new expressions of the human spirit, many drawing on universal themes, are being revealed in the modern leadlights that are finding their way into domestic and commercial venues all over the world.

The 30 original leadlight designs featured in this book, covering a wide range of subjects, are presented as a personal expression of the creative spirit, the result of thirteen years of experience in designing and making original leadlight windows.

My thanks to photographer John Endacott for his contribution to the book's photography pages, to those friends who have encouraged and aided me in my creative work, and to the Elizabeths, I and II.

All the designs included in this book are available, full-size, for a fee of $25, from the author's leadlight design service. Original new designs, drawn to your own individual needs and specifications, are also available for a fee.

Write outlining your requirements to:

Will Fraser, Leadlights, PO Box 36,
Hepburn Springs, Victoria 3461.

Birds

Zebra Finch

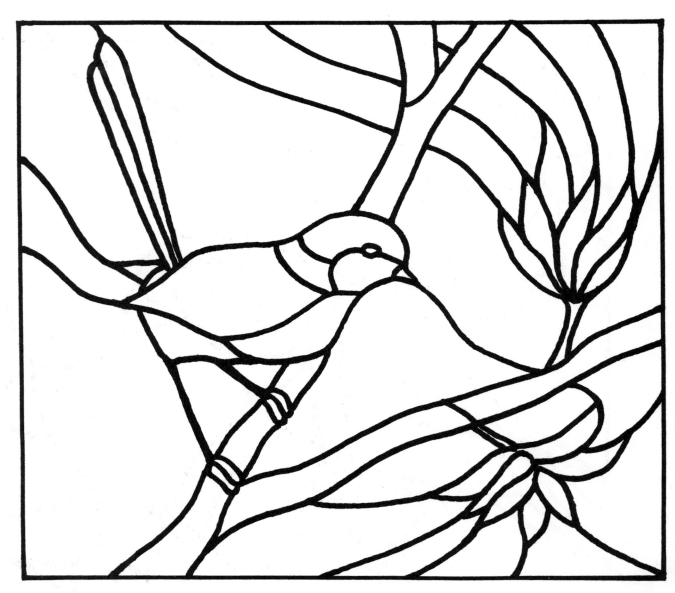

Purple-backed Wren

Magpie

Pale-headed Rosella

Rainbow Lorikeet

Galah

Crimson Rosellas

Barking Owl

Flowers

Foot of panel

Photographer: John Endacott

Photographer: John Endacott

Abstract Designs

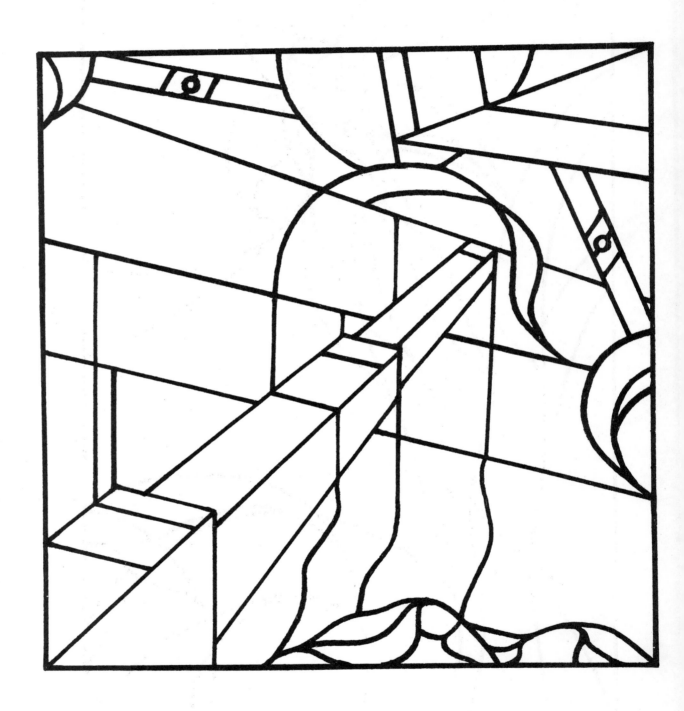

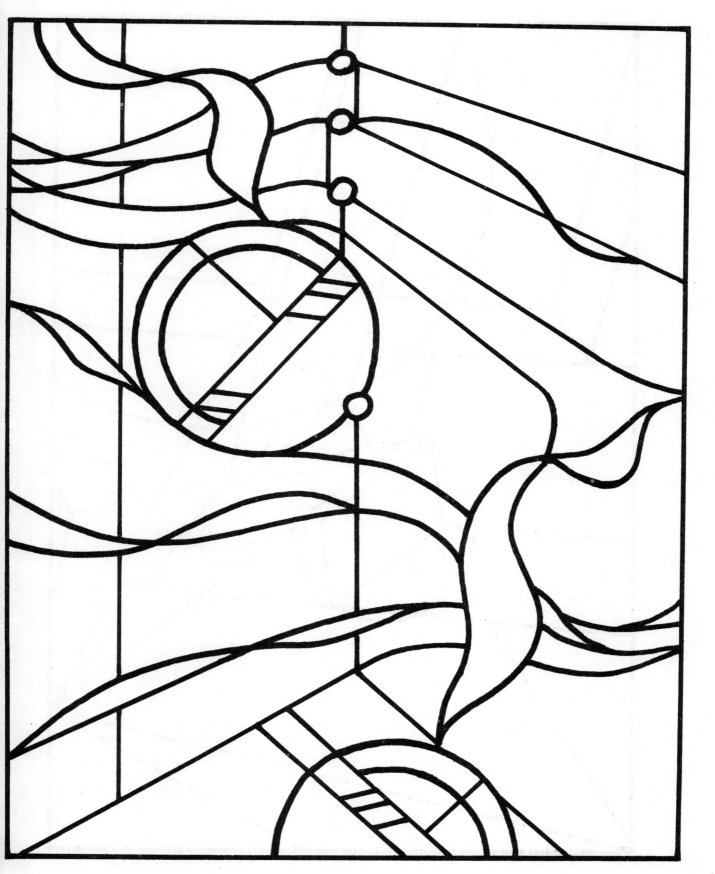

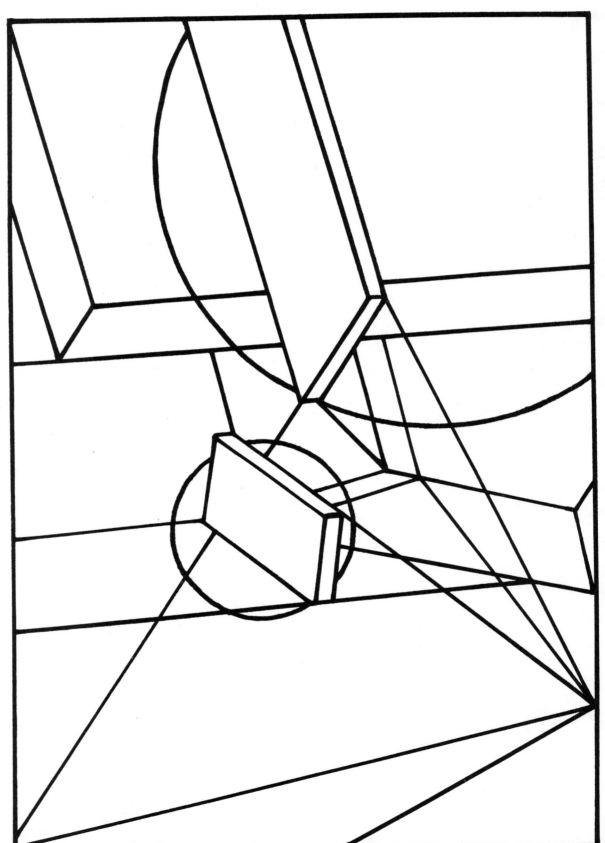

Foot of panel

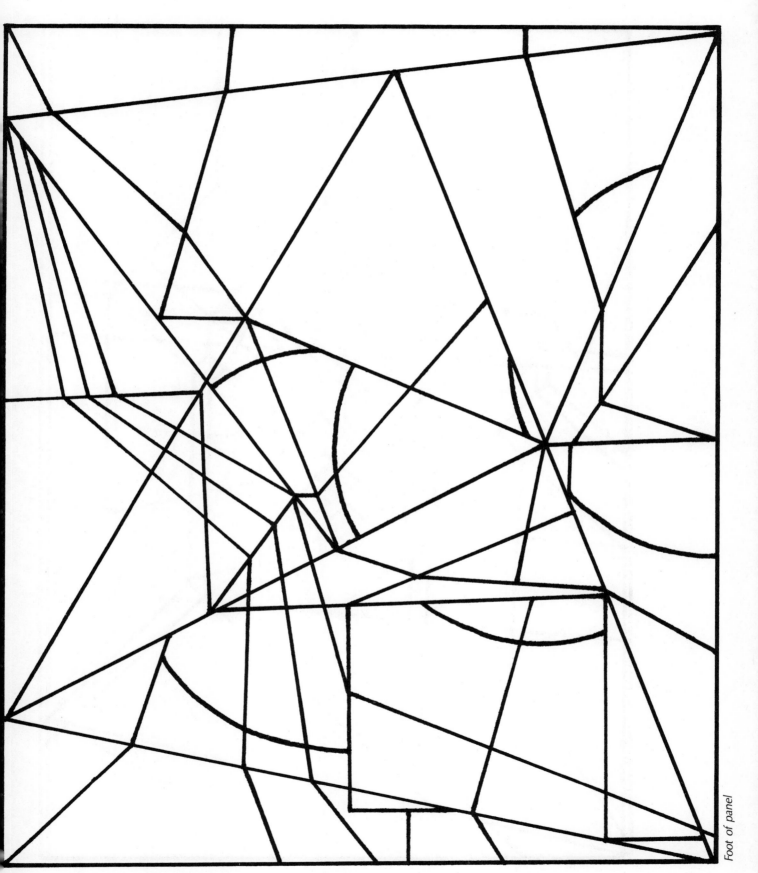

Foot of panel

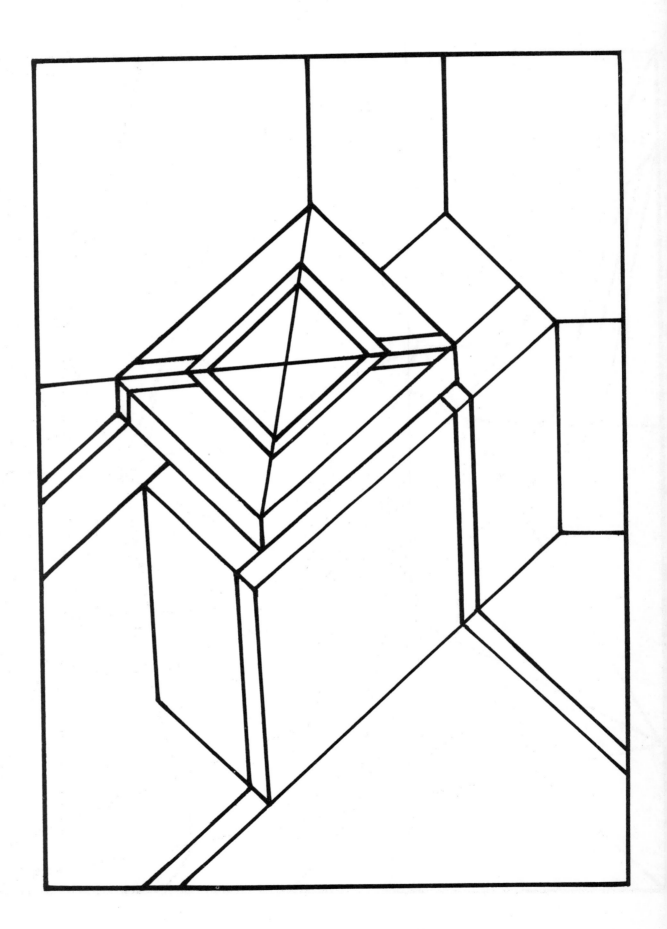

Landscapes

Foot of panel

Glass Suppliers

AUSTRALIA

Victoria
Briar Hill Stained Glass,
15 Sherbourne Road,
Briar Hill Vic. 3088

G. & H. Glassworks,
Cnr Rosella & New Sts,
Frankston Vic. 3199

Moorabbin Stained Glass,
2/16 Station Road,
Cheltenham Vic. 3192

Beverly Ross Leadlights,
Lot 3 Monbulk Road,
Kallista Vic. 3791

Southern Crafthouse,
477 Glenhuntly Road,
Elsternwick Vic. 3185

Art of Glass,
PO Box 732,
Mildura Vic. 3502

M.R. & A.T. Cameron,
62 Queens Parade,
Traralgon Vic. 3844

Glassworks Studio,
Benalla Road,
Shepparton East Vic. 3631

Mr Leadlights,
75 Mair Street East,
Ballarat Vic. 3350

Sale Stained Glass,
PO Box 913,
Sale Vic. 3850

South-West Aluminium and Glass,
30 Caramut Road,
Warrnambool Vic. 3280

Berwick Glass,
Lot 3 Enterprise Ave,
Berwick Vic. 3806

Chelsea Glass,
306 Nepean Highway,
Edithvale Vic. 3196

Honeysuckle Stained Glass,
2 Havilah Road,
Bendigo Vic. 3550

Pater Leadlights,
2 Power Road,
Bayswater Vic. 3153

Sapphire Glass & Glazing,
77 Bedford Road,
Ringwood Vic. 3134

S.R.A. Stained Glass,
535 High Street,
Echuca Vic. 3564

Stained Glass World,
929 Burke Road,
Camberwell Vic. 3124

Westcoast Leadlights,
130 Church Street,
Geelong North Vic. 3215

Williamstown Glazing,
221 Nelson Place,
Williamstown Vic. 3016

The Melbourne Glass Centre,
12–14 Ceylon Street,
Nunawading Vic. 3030
(Wholesale Only)

New South Wales
The Glass Connection,
Factory 1, 10 Norman Street,
Peakhurst NSW 2210
(Wholesale Only)

Albury Leadlights,
404 Macauley Street,
Albury NSW 2640

Spectrum Stained Glass &
Leadlights,
365 Concord Road,
Concord West NSW 2138

Sydney Stained Glass & Leadlights,
39 Pyrmont Street,
Pyrmont NSW 2009

Finn's Stained Glass,
129 Boundary Road,
Peakhurst NSW 2210

Bob Bush Leadlights,
102 Smith Street,
Summer Hill NSW 2130

Tiffany Glass Industries Pty Ltd,
Cnr. Harvey & Bowmans Roads,
Marayong NSW 2148

Smith's Glass Service, Leadlights,
481 Willoughby Road,
Willoughby NSW 2068

Penrose Glass,
272 Princes Highway,
Rockdale NSW 2216

Cherry Phillips,
27 Dunmore Street,
Croydon Park NSW 2133

Kensington Leadlights,
12 Lenthall Street,
Kensington NSW 2033

Studio 25 (Penrith),
Shop 2,
6 Bringelly Road,
Kingswood NSW 2747

Queensland
Hartley Williams & Co.,
PO Box 442,
Strathpine Qld. 4500
(Wholesale Only)

South Australia
The Adelaide Glass Centre,
20 College Road,
Kent Town SA 5067

Western Australia
The Colonial Stained Glass Works
220 Subiaco Road,
Subiaco WA 6008

Tasmania
Tasmanian Stained Glass,
'Blenheim', High Street,
Evandale Tas. 7212

UNITED STATES OF AMERICA

Arizona
Lincoln Distributors,
510 So. 52nd St, Suite 104,
Tempe AZ 85281

California
Franciscan Glass Co.,
100 San Antonio Circle,
Mt View CA 94040

Hollander Glass Co.,
10579 Dale,
Stanton CA 90680

Pacific Glass,
125 W. 157th Street,
Gardena CA 90248

Colorado
Artisans Wholesale,
666 Buchtel Blvd,
Denver CO 80210

D. & L. Stained Glass Co.,
4919 N. Broadway Space 40,
Boulder CO 80210

Georgia
Jennifers Glassworks,
PO Box 920556,
Norcross GA 30092

Mt Airy Glass Co. Inc.,
3670 Winsor Park Drive 6,
PO Box 158,
Suwanee GA 30174

Illinois
Hollander Glass Central,
630 Thomas Drive,
Bensenville IL 60106

Ed Hoy's International,
1620 Frontenac Road,
Naperville IL 60540

Massachusetts
Whittemore-Durgin,
825 Market St,
Rockland MA 02370
PO Box 2065,
Hanover MA 02339

New Jersey
Studio Design,
49 Shark River Road,
Neptune NJ 07753

S.A. Bendheim Co. Inc.,
61 Willett Street,
Passaic NJ 07055

New York
Hollander Glass East,
140 58th Street,
Brooklyn NY 11220

Ohio
Franklin Art Glass,
222 E. Sycamore Street,
Columbus OH 43206

Prism Art Glass,
111 W. Baird St,
6800 County Rd 189,
W. Liberty OH 43357

Oklahoma
Oklahoma Stained Glass,
8317 Gateway Terrace,
Oklahoma City OK 73149

Oregon
Cline Glass Company,
1135 SE Grand Avenue,
Portland OR 97214

Pennsylvania
The Glass Emporium,
322 S. Pennsylvania Ave,
North Wales PA 19454

South Carolina
Mt Airy Glass Co. Inc.,
PO Box 541, 205-B, S. Main St,
Greer SC 29652

Texas
Hollander Glass Texas,
9612 West Tidwell Road,
Houston TX 77041

Houston Stained Glass,
2420 Center,
Houston TX 77007

Washington
Northwest Art Glass,
9003 151st Ave, NE,
Redmond WA 98052

Big 'M' Stained Glass,
3201 4th Ave, South,
Seattle WA 98108

INTERNATIONAL GLASS DISTRIBUTORS

Canada
Glass Smith & Co.,
3311 Tennyson Avenue,
Victoria BC V8Z 3P5

Hollander Glass Canada,
3095 Universal Drive,
Mississauga Ontario L4X 2E2

Kaleido Glass Ltd,
2 Lamb Street,
Georgetown Ontario L7G 3M9

Kona Stained Glass Ltd,
1391 East 33rd Ave,
Vancouver BC V5V 3B9

Kona Stained Glass Ltd,
5, 204 Center Street North,
Sundre Alberta T0M 1X0

Tiffany Glass Centre,
7880 Alderbridge Way,
Richmond BC V6X 2A5

Japan
Juno Shoji Co. Inc.,
13-21 Chausumac
Moriyama-Ku, Nagoya

Tanaka & Co.,
1472 Hishie, Higashiosaka-City,
Osaka 578

Korea
Oh Yang Int'l Ltd,
CPO Box 5152,
Seoul

Mexico
Carlo International,
S.A. DE C.V.,
Cipres No. 1440 COL. Morelos,
44910, Guadalajara, Jal. Mexico

Carlo International,
S.A. DE C.V.,
AV 1 No. 36 San Pedro De Los
Pinos,
Mexico, D.F. Mexico

Egypt
Universal Arts & Crafts,
P.O. Box 777,
Maadi, Cairo

New Zealand
Smith & Smith Glass,
173 Captain Springs Road,
Onehunga, Auckland

Chevalier Leadlighting,
130 Kitchener Road,
Milford

Feilding Stained Glass Studio
P.O. Box 526,
Feilding

England
Kansa Craft,
The Flour Mill, Wath Rd,
Elsecar, Barnsley,
South Yorkshire S748ET

Stained Glass Supplies,
Unit 5, Brunel Way,
Thornbury Industrial Estate,
Thornbury, Avon

Holland
Smit Tools BV,
Radboudweg 3,
3911 BE-Rhenen-Netherlands
PO Box 126
3910 AC-Rhenen-Netherlands

Italy
A.T.V. s.r.l.
Via Charta 77, 14
50018 Scandicci Florence

Spain
Taller Ideriero SA,
c/o Peru No. 80 (interior)
03800 Alcoy (Alicante)

Switzerland
Creative Glass,
Seefeldstr. 186,
8008 Zurich

Turkey & Cyprus
LIBRA Dis Ticaret/
Foreign Trade LTD,
Refik Saydam Cad 191/3
Sishane 80050, Istanbul

West Germany
Crysopal,
Barkauer Str. 119,
D2300 Kiel I

EDDI American Glass
GmbH,
Dieselstrasse 30,
5600 Wuppertal 22

KPL Kunst und Technic,
Huttensee Str. 40,
D-7995 Neukirch

Karl Wirtz
Aluwir,
Germaniastr. 39,
4600 Dortmund 70 (Marten)

Karl Wirtz,
Filiale Sud,
Max Eythstr. 3,
7049 Steinenbronn

Tiffany Glaskunst GmbH,
Hellefort Str. 18,
4815 Schloss-Holte Stukenbrock